SITE CONTROL

America's Secret Swamp

MELVIN PRINCE JOHNAKIN JR.

SITE CONROL

America's Secret Swamp

Copyright 2021 by Melvin Prince Johnakin Jr.

First Edition: [December 2020]
Printed in the United States of America

Table of Contents

DEDICATION

To everyone who needs a voice… this one's for you!

Dedicated to my niece; Tamesha A. Johnakin a schoolteacher in the Philadelphia Public School system. She shared with me that there is probably no group in the United States that needs more critical assistance than Black Americans. Their relatively fragile state of family life, the problems of illegitimacy, unsupervised rearing of children, school conditions, community maintenance, "crime in the streets," and so on, call out for serious attention in all welfare organizations.

To an increasing extent White leader are realizing that these handicaps have been largely inflicted upon Blacks by Whites and that responsibility for their amelioration should be a community wide concern regardless of color.

Thanks, I am very proud to have a very woke niece!

My book Site Control is in part Dedicated to Dr. Gregory Smith one of the best Professors at the historical Cheyney University, the first HBCU. He reminds all Cheyney students, "Our values are so much an intrinsic part of our lives and behavior that we are often unaware of them or, at least, we are unable to think about them clearly and articulately. Yet our values, along with other factors, clearly determine our choices, as can be proved by presenting individuals with equally 'reasonable' alternate possibilities and comparing the choices they make. Some will choose one course, others another, and each will feel that his or her election is the rational one."

By William Guthrie and Renato Tagiuri
"Personal Values and Corporate Strategy"

FOREWORD

Those who believe systemic or institutional racism does not exist are not privy to the inner workings of Unions. Nor how the very construct as a nonprofit entity touches every aspect of infrastructure in our daily life: from the exterior of the house, interior, insurance, and site control. They are in every crevice of society and seemingly run the world.

Site Control, hmm? What is the significance, and who controls what? This process and arena are only for the highly shrewd; skilled wordsmiths who are proficient in negotiations and exceptional in executing, and I do not mean those with a physical trade or day laborers. But individuals, groups, and organizations with strong leadership that knows the game, make the rules, and determine who participates and are ruthless when it comes to acquiring first-position, which is everything. Although the intricacies and methodologies aren't new to the blocking that occurs, just now far more sophisticated in its execution and shrouded in FANCY language and endless requirements designed to keep "other folks" out. Nevertheless, the process is equally as brutal as when staking one's claim for land meant fighting by any means necessary, and I will get more into that a little later.

However, in our current day, we have more rules, governance, and individuals strategically positioned as wedges to control manufacturing, building, and development that determines market vitality and expansion in every industry. The turf war is serious.

The very fabric of the United States is controlled by a few individuals that belong to groups, and some in those groups are heads of organizations that are made bosses who rule with brute strength to ensure the path for their next generation is paved with golden parachutes, and uninterrupted cash flow. It's akin to Chattel Slavery. And no matter how much others outside of their organizations dream of taking a stake in the industry, or to change the trajectory that could diminish their net proceeds, it is a futile attempt that is met with primal force. There are layers of protection infused to nip it in the bud or annihilate the new game in town from trying to surface. But certainly, they never give up Site Control. Many have tried to dethrone the movement, but none has ever succeeded, not even some in the United States government.

Also, the notion of getting to the top in some industries without the blessing of these rulers is mythological. The path is depicted; there is a formula, and it is not predicated on being fair or sharing the spoil... One of many takeaways from this book demonstrates the connectivity of the law-abiding and the lawless, and sometimes you find both eating from the same table and joined at the hip through Site Control.

CHAPTER 1

SOME NEED NOT APPLY

Site Control is similar to the jostling by whites against nonwhites dating back to the 1800s for control of land given by the United States government as part of the Homestead Act. During this period individuals were allowed to file claims for open land owned by the government to help settle the land. Those who successfully submitted their claims promptly and were without *wrongdoings* against the United States during the time of war were given consideration and some granted land.

This was a very *intricate* investment by the U.S. government to help advance the development and expansion of the country, and a paradigm by which many ordinances became the *decree* and rules of operation for the newly emerging agencies. It is the same process that exists today and is designed to marginalize and block others from profiting from any business transaction with the government and private industry that involves certain trades. The **powers-that-be** have already created the *charter* by which business will come in, be processed, and assigned accordingly, and if you do not fit into one of their pre-approved groups, forget about it! This has been and still is a contested battle for equality and inclusion and we have a long way to go before the ratio increases to represent a fair share of participation.

For clarity, there were several Acts created and implemented in the 1800s that gave Whites and a few Blacks a head start. It is imperative to expound a little more and not induce too much deviation, but to assist with laying a foundation of how we got here it is necessary to include the backstory.

The Homestead Act was numerous laws in the United States by which an applicant could file and acquire ownership of government land or public domains, also referenced as a homestead. So, in principle, we see some of the exact processes still ruling and blocking individuals from partaking in various industries because of what is "First Position"; Site Control.

The Homestead Act of 1866 was all-inclusive: Black Americans and women were explicitly included and could apply; they were encouraged to do so just as long as an applicant had not taken up arms against the Federal government of the United States. However, Whites felt Blacks and women, in particular, should not be equal to them. Blacks should be an *addendum*, sub, not a prime applicant and certainly should not be considered a primary applicant to establish any collateral that would give them more economic power than some of the lesser unfortunate White counterparts or create a position whereby they were considered equal in economic value. Therefore, discrimination and systemic barriers forced a slow down for Blacks on the homestead.

Now let us keep in mind there were several Acts, and some had *fewer* requirements than others, but Whites, especially Southern Whites were determined to annihilate any possibilities of Negroes getting ahead and making money, and definitely not to become landowners. After all, if they succeeded where would the free or low paid laborer come from? Unequivocally, we cannot glance over the mindset of paying less and getting more has not disappeared, though the Homestead Act is not the prize possession today with the Government.

However, procurement opportunities and contracts are, and just like the mentality of many narrow-minded family leaders who fought vigorously to snuff out any chances for Blacks and all non-Whites to participate equally, the battle yet goes on in the 21st Century... It's now controlled by labor unions.

The scoop or skinny that profited generations from granddad, dad, son, uncle, nephew now includes mom, sister, nieces, wives, and girlfriends. I knew that would raise your curiosity but more to come that will not disappoint. Let us take into consideration the business arena once perceived as a hardnose playground for gritty means transformed into a construct whereby women were now the tool to taint the pool. The intent was to keep out non-Whites... can you not see the fence with the sign "Under Construction- Keep Out?" Danger!

This book is an exemplary illustration and discourse on how the U.S. economic system is rigged and structured to prevent participation at the highest, most lucrative levels. And with this understanding, the objective is to enlighten and provide a fresh perspective to a process many are overwhelmed by, and no matter what your education level, there is NO way to move and thrive in this arena without the NOD. The bedfellows are intertwined in a love-hate relationship that is held airtight only by transactions; a process by which some get power, stay in power, and control power. **SITE CONTROL.**

Also, the other hypocrisy is many in the game are legally and constitutionally disqualified to participate, but when the scepter is extended, life is always given.

Purportedly anyone with a federal record is not qualified to participate in federal contracts; the upstanding FEDS seek those with squeaky clean backgrounds and possess strong work ethics. At least that is what the paperwork suggests . . . In writing, government contracts or grants require an applicant not to have any felonies against the U.S. government. Now, we all know somewhere a few rotten apples were still left in the basket...

If contractors are found to have submitted false information on previous applications, they can be barred from any further engagement at the infancy level and that is also equally important because you have to have a flow of information. This industry is not governed by luck, the flow of information, and knowing the players makes the possibility real or keeps it dormant as a dream with no legs to grow.

As you can imagine for there to be legal ACTS and hundreds of manuals on governance there had to be and is anticipated will be many acts of theft, and criminality. They go hand-in-hand. Though just out of curiosity are we to believe the existing models in the *"TRADE"* industry are governed by those with the highest ethics? A question, not a presumption. And if the first is true then one could conclude that every

Black and Brown contractor/subcontractor who could never get access to open bids, or even after getting a bid has all the tools provided in writing to successfully submit a bid and therefore are/were discounted, DENIED, and labeled unqualified. You can label with many adjectives and not all would be true or applicable.

So, just out of curiosity are we to believe that all existing *Prime Contractors* in the Trades and Procurement who successfully win bid after-bid, are the most honest? And do those often rejected, blocked, or denied such as Blacks and Latinas somehow are representative of an element of untruth?

False Claims Act

One of the most common ways that a contractor can be barred from submitting bids on local, state, or federal government public works projects is because the contractor is accused of submitting a false claim in violation of the state or federal False Claims Act. False Claims Act violations arise when a contractor submits a request for payment on a public project that includes exaggerated amounts for materials, labor, or services. These violations can also occur when a contractor does not perform work under the material terms of the contract or provide defective work. These violations also arise when a contractor procures a contract by fraud such as by overstating qualifications or claiming to have licenses that they do not have.

Have you ever wondered how big builders get contracts, where and how they got started? What type of network is required to have a conversation, to be invited to a social function or leisurely trek the globe golfing, sailing, or attend some other kind of high-stake fun outing?

Perhaps you grew up dreaming to play in this arena as you admired skyscrapers and communities being built and thought you'd become an architect, engineer, or painter because you have an eye for pulling beautiful things together and sought out to qualify for your ONE DAY. See until it happens it is all ONE DAY... One day you will know, one day you'll get the contracts, one day your firm will host events for the underprivileged as a way to show your gratitude for finally arriving. But what does the journey consist of concerning getting to score that ONE DAY?

Let's take a look at the perils/disadvantages/perks/cushions in the building TRADES and PROCUREMENT. Although a Brown or Black baby is born equally to a White baby, naked, and totally dependent, and possibly two parents who believe the best will manifest for them. They can all grow up to share the identical vision to build things, to be a PRIME, but only 1 of the 3 will have a path of least resistance, and the latter 2 will face insurmountable obstacles just submitting a bid.

Well, even before the submission process there was a time in American history getting information about open bids or forthcoming projects were the biggest hurdles. NO information, No opportunity. And so, it was for a very long-time people of color who were cut out from the inception even on small projects like framing, painting, caulking, maintenance, security, and don't ever think about site control.

From the outside looking into the world of the progressive business types who seemingly have everything together; multiple homes, cars, favorite vacation spots, investments, children doing okay, and a loving home, were fine pillars in the community always willing to give a hand to those in need, and some of the biggest charitable donors. But many also perpetuated one of the biggest cons, helping poor people.

Well, by the description, none would think, where did the money come from. At any rate, let us delve into the nuances of dealing with big Business, Education, Law Enforcement, building trade, and the lie of apprenticeship as the golden scepter of passage to get in the game.

If you ever heard the deck is stacked against you, believe it. There is so much to uncover from OSHA, that within itself is a treasure trove of restrictions and readily suitable language to deny, block, and eliminate participation.

CHAPTER 2

Apprenticeship

Let us take the guesswork out of how you get started; What is APPRENTICESHIP?

And who is connected and why? To answer the latter of the 2 questions first, the winners are:

Laborers International Union of North America;

1. International Association of Bridges, Structural, Ornamental and Reinforcing Iron Workers;

2. International Association of Heat and Frost Insulators and Allied Workers *(est. 1903) considered Energy Conservation Specialists;*

3. International Union of Elevator Constructors *(organized in*

1901);

4. United Brotherhood of Carpenters and Joiners of America

5. International Union of Bricklayers and Allied Craftworkers - Shipbuilders – Blacksmiths -Forgers & Helpers [IBB] *founded in 1880.*

The Unions influence, control and govern what procedures are implemented in skilled labor and service operations that utilize specialized craftsmanship and it should be understood that the ORDER, or brotherhood, is a close-knit community where dissension is frowned upon not just figuratively, but even to the extent of possible inflicting bodily harm or obstructing business transactions: The ORDER will shut you down!

Unequivocally, this is real raw power with sophisticated methodologies and integrated into the business, health, educational, entertainment and service corridors in the entire world. That is a lot of juice. Unions' long-standing rule in the trades depicts its ability to maneuver, influence, deny, and control the operations of businesses. At a glimpse, let us look at IBB (International Brotherhood of Boilermakers).

The International Brotherhood of Boilermakers grew out of the Industrial Revolution and the demand for steam power. Organized in 1880, it is one of the oldest unions in the United States. And has more than 200 local lodges across North America.

What is a Boilermaker? The Organization describes itself as:

"We're the skilled craftsmen and women trained and committed to stand apart as the best in rigging, welding, and other specialty crafts. We step up when others step back, completing the jobs others are afraid to begin. We solve the hardest problems. And we're the choice for owners and contractors who want the job done right—on time, within budget, and safely. Every time.

We're a brotherhood. And everything we are begins with our bond. That's our advantage."

However, at the end of the day, there is ONE primary presence involved in all Union activity, OSHA.

OSHA's footprint is seen in every transaction from the paper from which contracts are printed, chairs and desks occupied in offices with oversight of job sites around the world, to the food or craft services that supply cafeterias and restaurants where its members work, and the list goes on and on.

So, the million-dollar question remains how does one participate? What do you need to do first?

One of the many building blocks to participating in the colossal arena with Unions and Trades starts with getting an APPRENTICESHIP. Though notice it is not the "ONLY" approach or means by which one gets to earn a living with unions. However, if you aspire to own and operate a private business and desire to qualify for the bidding process to participate as a sub or Prime on government contracts or even in the private sector, without question having had an apprenticeship provides many advantages.

When you learn the value and benefits of contractual acquisitions that too few are cognizant of, this is the golden hen that never stops laying.

The subtle but cherished dissemination of information sets businesses apart from the rest; knowing what is available and how to *partak*e is the difference between a weekly salary and the Prime who makes millions. And most Primes are the gatekeepers that get to make many unspoken rules of engagement. They let you in or challenge your participation but make no mistake they have real POWER and loyal lucrative relationships by which families and generations are sustained. It is the other family outside of the biological realm, but with many affinities and willingness to protect by any means necessary.

There are pros and cons for both the employer and employee.

PROS

PRACTICAL EXPERIENCE

You have the opportunity to gain valuable practical experience in your chosen field. Gaining experience whilst working towards a qualification allows you to build up a respectable CV and ensure that everything that you're learning will be relevant to your career.

EARN WHILE YOU LEARN

Earning money while earning a qualification is definitely positive. Being motivated by money may mean that an apprenticeship would be more appropriate than a university as you can start earning from the get-go. The current national minimum wage for apprentices under 19 is $26.00 an hour, although many firms pay more than this.

NO DEBT

This speaks for itself; you can go into life after your apprenticeship debt-free.

LEARN ON THE JOB

Apprentices learn on the job, building up knowledge and skills, gaining qualifications, and earning money all at the same time. You work towards a work-based qualification such as a National Vocational Qualification (NVQ) which is recognized by employers all over the country.

CONS

YOU CANNOT GAIN ACCESS TO CERTAIN CAREERS THROUGH AN APPRENTICESHIP ROUTE BY MISSING OUT ON THE UNIVERSITY EXPERIENCE.

Having an undergraduate degree is an essential requirement for certain careers, particularly in arears such as medicine and science.

DIVERSITY EXPERIENCE

For many, the university isn't just about getting a degree, it's about moving to a new place, meeting new people, and having a good time – shocking, I know. So, by doing an apprenticeship, you have to plunge straight into the world of work which may take a hit on your social life.

RESPONSIBILITY

Some might feel overwhelmed at first. Your employer will have deadlines to meet and clients to please. This can be a steep learning curve and it is important to take things seriously.

It is important to remember that everyone is different and what works for you may not work for other people. Different careers and employers have different specifications. Some may value experience over qualification or a good attitude.

Apprenticeship is a learning environment that empowers you to gain invaluable skill sets and acquire other strategic attributes to develop the emotional capacity to work with others, to learn how to take and execute orders, and how to create best practices. This process is fundamental and could be an asset. All Primes master these fundamental qualities which enable them to participate in high paying contracts. Let us face it, nobody gambles billions on a novice… Knowledge, experience, and having great relationships are priceless and required. An Apprenticeship could provide a glimpse into this process.

Also, it is paramount to keep in mind that having an Apprenticeship opportunity is essential to expanding global financial markets because not everyone is suited for ivy league institutions or a 9-5. And individuals who are equipped to own and run private businesses represent a strategic role to ensure participation and opportunities whereby industries could continue to thrive.

However, when it comes to privately owned business participation in private/government contracts at the highest level, the engagement pulls back the curtain to a whole other world of primal instinct and it is not that easy.

There are national programs funded by the government with objectives to ensure America not only has a ready workforce, but a skilled and learned job pool. Take a look at one of many funded programs like PACA [Philadelphia Apprenticeship Coordinators Association).

What is paramount and imperative to recognize is there is a formula to participate with Unions. No matter how one may want to play his or her cards independently, there is NO such thing in the trades because it is Union ruled, Union protected, and the UNION has already defined the parameters of engagement of its members. And the many benefits of Apprenticeship guarantee the Unions will continue to grow intellectually and maintain their power through paid membership, and influence with legislative representation.

Disadvantages of apprenticeships for employers

- Time Consuming – Taking the time to teach an apprentice your trade, is certainly going to slow you down, even meaning in the short-term you can take on less work

- Lack of Commercial Understanding – As well as a lack of experience, often you might find that apprentices lack the commercial understanding of working within the trade.

It is best to take the time to consider your options since most employers place a higher value on graduates.

Benefits

- Described as structured training programs designed to help you acquire the know-how and skills needed to help you achieve success within your chosen line of work, apprenticeships provide participants with the opportunity to work in practical situations to earn a qualification.

- You get to advance much faster through your chosen career by securing a job earlier. Furthermore, you get to make a handsome amount of money earlier in life.

- By hitting the ground running through participation in apprenticeships, you demonstrate to employers that you are ready to work; more importantly, you get to earn some much-needed experience. You also get to gain huge amounts of confidence in your line of work by participating in a hands-on learning program.

- Apprenticeships ensure that you are earning a salary while under training. Since you get a paycheck from your employer, while the government covers tuition payments, as is the case for most students, you can forget about paying tuition and accumulating student loans.

- It facilitates freedom of choice. With over 400 apprenticeships available in a variety of industries including commerce, construction, sales, and sports among others; finding an opportunity in your desired line of work will be easy.

- It is a different approach to learning. By participating in apprenticeships, you get to spend your learning time working as opposed to studying all day.

- It entails, learning from experienced heads in the same workplace, such as Journeymen, and through hands-on training. This also allows you to earn further qualifications including HNDs and HNCs as well as honorary and foundation degrees.

CHAPTER 3

IT IS EVERYWHERE

Any time there is Site Control it is common practice to implement mandatory minimum Judicial laws that could involve some level of evacuation, mask-wearing, or compliance that could shut down businesses, schools, and essential infrastructure such as roads, bridges, etc. There is a tremendous amount of power that an institution or organization can wield that could have long-lasting economic and social implications.

For instance, under the current pandemic, mayors and governors have the right to take control of operations of schools, businesses, and roads; it is a different process of site control, but it is site control. Though governors have the power to override mayoral decisions, normally this does not happen unless the trajectory imposed by a mayor is not in the best interest of mitigating or resolving an existing problem. And as you will discover this is not an arena for NOVICES to be in the driver's seat.

Key elements that must be in place:

Unequivocally, there is no substitute for experience and know how, especially in construction, but we will explore a few other trades as well. Years of experience in building projects, managing employees, working with owners, hiring subcontractors, keeping positive cash flow coming in, and tackling daily issues as they arise all help mold a person into an expert in their field. Even if you enter this arena as a consultant. The more exposure you have, the difficulty that is experienced where you have to not only resolve issues but also create innovative processes that benefit the entirety of the project makes you an invaluable asset.

There are 5 key areas in Site Control where you must have proven, successful leadership:

1. **Management**

2. **Legal**

3. **Employees**

4. **Safety**

5. **Sales**

Each of these areas requires experience and it is not relegated to construction. If you own and/or operate a restaurant, hair salon, car wash, retail store, school, or law firm, just examples with no significance in the order of listing, all require having a great management *team*. Not just ownership, a dictator, or passive-aggressive manager spewing orders where folks walk around on eggshells.

The management "team" is essential to the success of the project and should consist of self-starters who are knowledgeable. Team members should be interchangeable in certain areas but as a "whole" those who follow directions and add to the intellectual components of operations. In addition, the one at the top must be people-oriented with a skill set to delegate, and visionary to consistently expand operations, which can only be achieved with an effective management team.

Many hold to a leadership style of just having an enthusiastic aggressive sales team or leader as the *only* key to being successful... These traits are necessary, but nothing replaces people skills.

The benefits cannot/should not be underestimated because enthusiasm can carry a meeting when things begin to go awry. The ability to solve problems can help you create solutions to satisfy customers' needs. Listening carefully to customers demonstrates your investment in their success and shows understanding. Assertiveness can move a sales situation forward without offending or frustrating customers when tactfully implemented. All of which should be kept in mind as you build out and expand with Site Control.

When you see Site Control you should look for:

1. Leadership Skills. ...
2. Organizational Skills. ...

3. *Excellent Written and Verbal Communication.* ...
4. *Intelligence.* ...
5. *Active Listening Skills.* ...
6. *Honesty, Ambition, and a Strong Work Ethic*

Other intricate components of Site Control have everything to do with your legal team. LEGAL is one of the most vital partnerships you will need and cannot afford to omit to invest in securing the best and the brightest with vast experience. If you are looking to reduce cost, this is not the line item where you should do this. It is imperative to acquire the services of an experienced legal firm with relationships with the legislature. Government relations is a huge part of Site Control.

Your legal team is responsible for creating well-defined contracts that protect you and are the foundation of your organization. Conflict disagreements with owners, subcontractors, and material suppliers can manifest in long-drawn-out situations that can cost considerable time and money and possibly undo your project. Unresolved issues/concerns could shut your doors. So be sure to invest in LEGAL, and only take on a legal time with measurements. Make sure you have a legal team that's forward-thinking, engaging, and on top of laws that are constantly changing as well as regulations are put in place.

There are 12 essential professions we cannot do without to function effectively in the 21st Century, and some are restricted professions that must be protected and invested in to keep our society moving forward and yes, many are a part of Site Control.

The 12 occupations that are identified as vital to keeping our country running are:

1. Farmers, Ranchers, and other Agricultural Managers

Number employed: 494,879
Median income: $30,597

Why we cannot live without them: Farms produce the crops and livestock that represent most, if not all, of the food found in our pantries and refrigerators.

2. Water and Wastewater Treatment Plant and System Operators

Number employed: 113,370
Median income: $45,968

Why we cannot live without them: Water and wastewater workers are responsible for the constant monitoring, cleaning, and frequent testing of water samples. Without these workers, we wouldn't have the easy access to fresh water that we all enjoy.

3. Teachers

Number employed: 4,031,658
Median income: $55,557

Why we cannot live without them: Teachers play a vital role in giving our children knowledge, while also preparing them to become successful adults.

4. Construction Laborers

Number employed: 1,335,944
Median income: $31,658

Why we cannot live without them: Construction workers are responsible for building our cities and communities. They build bridges, skyscrapers, houses, and just about everything else.

5. Electrical and Telecommunications Line Installers and Repairers

Number employed: 238,922
Median income: $60,965

Why we cannot live without them: We rely on electronic devices today more than ever. These workers are responsible for maintaining the cable lines that keep our electricity and phone lines up and running.

6. Refuse and Recyclable Material Collectors

Number employed: 134,250
Median income: $34,258

Why we cannot live without them: Without these workers, our streets and neighborhoods would be overrun with garbage. Research from Yale University revealed that Americans throw out 5 pounds of trash per person, every day.

7. Police and Sheriffs Patrol Officers

Number employed: 675,939
Median income: $60,466

Why we cannot live without them: Police officers help keep us safe. They maintain order and respond to emergency situations whenever they are called upon.

8. Firefighters

Number employed: 314,928
Median income: $48,859

Why we cannot live without them: Firefighters keep communities safe from one of the most vicious natural forces on the planet. Research from the National Fire Protection Association discovered that fires were responsible for 3,275 civilian deaths and $11.5 billion in property damage in 2014.

9. EMTs, Paramedics, and Ambulance Drivers

Number employed: 266,853
Median income: $32,510

Why we cannot live without them: These workers save lives on a daily basis by providing emergency medical treatment and patient transportation to medical facilities.

10. Registered Nurses

Number employed: 2,870,340
Median income: $69,077

Why we cannot live without them: From hospitals and doctor's offices to nursing homes and home care, nurses are what keeps most medical operations running *smoothly. They interact with patients even more than doctors and provide the type of hands-on care most patients require.*

11. Military Occupations

Number employed: 2,098,652
Median income: $35,194

Why we cannot live without them: These men and women protect Americans on a daily basis. Whether it is operating in combat or training capacities, or providing essential services like transportation, medical care, and legal assistance, the U.S. military has enough professions to ensure our safety in any situation.

12. Heavy and Tractor-trailer Truck Drivers

Number employed: 1,926,886
Median income: $39,312

Why we cannot live without them: These workers are responsible for delivering the goods and services our citizens buy and sell each day. Most products and packages are driven on trucks between cities, states, or even cross-country.

You should be able to distinguish the importance of site control in each of the aforementioned industries, and the role Unions play, and why it is paramount to ensure your legal and management team are individuals who are committed to not only making money but impacting society.

Chapter 4

The Purpose of Site Control

If you plan to own or operate a business where there is public traffic the governance of Site Control will impact you. Though we are more familiar with having to meet the requirements set by OSHA and LABOR, which is simply SITE CONTROL.

Unequivocally Site Control is a huge component in every industry. There are set formulas and principles that govern the operations and ensures protection for workers, the community, and the environment.

The initial purpose of Site Control is not primarily to pad exclusive benefits for Unions; the broader scope is to abate possible contamination of workers, or the public from health hazards, and prevent theft of property or other sorts of vandalism. In addition, Site Control controls the activities and movement of people, equipment, and money. The latter affects every household in America regarding taxes or direct services.

Aspects of Site Control

Any construction site under development will have what is called a Site Map, which is created to give a visual of the entirety of the project and its assets. A construction site map is not to be confused with a *Site Map* for web Domains which is used to develop content and help users find and navigate large, complex sites by showing the entirety of the structure. Although you can see some functionalities are the same: to guide and display the assets with which you have to work with to achieve your objective.

A Site Map varies by project size and functionality. What is designed for Skyscrapers is not the same construct for the neighborhood bakery, carwash, or salon. However, what is similar is the application to identify any hidden infrastructure if the buildout entails installing water lines, gas lines, electrical conduits, or other infrastructure components.

SIGNIFICANCE

You have to know where every infrastructural connection is located: electric, gas, or if chemical tanks or other hazardous materials are on site. A Site Map sounds like a fancy process but actually, it is designed to guide in the build-out of an operation.

Also, a site map will show topographic features, if a high rise is the project, knowing the prevailing wind direction and velocity during certain times of the season is paramount. As well as the efficacy of drainage which also determines the best placement of the front or back of a building.

One other critical aspect of Site Maps is that they are always or should be a work in progress. The Site Map should change as the progress and structural progression takes place, which means the Site Management team must be thorough to provide updates as information changes.

Since the Site Map is fluid listed below are several areas that will need to be reflected:

- Accidents
- Emergencies
- New materials not originally used at the site
- Vandalism
- Changes in site activities
- Weather

Other usages for a Site Map are:

- Planning

- Assigning personnel

- Identifying access routes, evacuation routes, and problem areas

- Identifying areas of the Site that require use of personal protective equipment

- Supplementing the daily safety and health briefings of the field teams.

The Map should be prepared prior to Site entry and updated throughout the course of the site operations.

In any industry there are set formulas and principles that governs the operation and could include a vast array of disciplines or trades. It could be something as simple as operating a food stand, or a bicycle shop, though vastly different yet each are connected to one simple common denominator: Unions. The food stand operator's food is handled by one or more trades: Agricultural and trucking or rail so here we have the Boilers Union and Food Services as silent partners, not to provide monetary support but governance.

Site Control for larger projects consist of development of several key zones, and each are immensely different in functionality.

Work Zone Types

➢ **Evacuation:** Exit strategy

➢ **Command Post:** Supervision of all field operations and field teams.

- ➢ **Exclusion Zone:** The area where contamination does or could occur.

- ➢ **Contamination Reduction Zone:** The transition area between the contaminated area and the clean area.

- ➢ **Support Zone:** The location of the administrative and other support functions needed to keep the operations in the Exclusion and Contamination Reduction Zones running smoothly.

- ➢ **Medical Station:** Self-explanatory (First aide – Medical)

- ➢ **Equipment and Supply Centers:** Supply, maintenance, and repair of communications, respiratory, and sampling equipment.

- ➢ **Administration:** Interface with home office on all aspects of the Site.

- ➢ **Field Laboratory** Coordination and processing of environmental and hazardous waste samples.

- ➢ **The Buddy System:** To provide information and assistance to his or her partner.

- ➢ **Site Security:** To prevent the exposure of unauthorized, unprotected people to site hazards.

- ➢ **Communication Systems:** Two sets of communication systems should be established; internal communication among personnel on site, and external communication between onsite and offsite personnel.

Each of the aforementioned represents a critical component that could impact deliverables and there is no skimping on intellect or skill set; the success of the project is dependent on who is in control and every project must have an experienced Project Manager or Site Manager, and strong Site Control Program. The bigger the project, the more experience is required.

In addition, Planning is paramount and essential to your deliverables and business model; the degree of Site Control will vary based on Site features, Site sizes, and the environment or community.

Knowing which phases to implement is established in the Site Control program which should always be established in the planning phase, and modified as new information, Site materials or environmental changes happen.

Chapter 5

The Impact

Site Control covers a broad range of services and industries including social services that impact over 5 million of America's poor. Predominantly, the poor living in Public Housing.

Extensive research conducted by John Goering a professor of Public Affairs at the School of Public Affairs of Baruch College and at the Graduate Center of the City University of New York denoted numerous disconnects and anomalies with the quality-of-life residents integrated into the Moving to Opportunity (MTO) Demonstration. Several studies conducted on MTO policies shows that poverty in the United States is increasingly concentrated in *"high-poverty"* neighborhoods, and residents in those areas are still less likely to break the cycles of poverty despite the availability of support services: childcare, employment training, and retention, educational services, entrepreneurial education, and homeownership programs. One could ask what connection poverty has in association with Site Control; all of the above services are connected to Unions. And Union labor encompasses Site Control. There is not one service provider without Union affiliation, so the question becomes;

is there a design whereby people, poor people are flooded into a pipeline of services that leads to nowhere?

Unequivocally, there is no incentive for millions to vacate a system that guarantees the provision of basic necessities and will sometimes look the other way when income thresholds are violated; there are no house checks unless someone files a complaint, or the police are called. The concept of Public Housing created and continues to promote a subgroup of negating factors that deteriorates the core of human advancement and squashes ingenuity and induced biopsychosocial ruin where families and individuals are/were unable to fully grasp the psychological clutches that block progression.

This system is propped up by taxpayers and the gatekeepers and bosses, particularly white males both in government and the private sector, systematically profit from this biopsychosocial disconnection in less educated and poor Black and Brown people. A few Blacks are given some status to ensure the commodity doesn't diminish by being cognizant and develop ingenuity to leave the fields of no return.

In 1935, the first federally funded Public Housing project was created. America has over 160 years in the Public Housing business; it is not just a social service; it is a colossal business entity. But the last 75 years up to the present, does not show a decline, but unfortunately, the very opposite. Public Housing is a booming economy of its own. It is big business where billions are passed, and folks are made rich. However, at the bottom rung are the poor, uneducated, physical, or mentally challenged that are the pawns for the continuation of certain services and contracts. Without question as a civilized society, there should be measures in place to support the less fortunate as well as there should be an investment in higher education or vocational training to challenge, inspire, and coach individuals to move forward. When one loses, the collective loses.

It is important to point out that Public Housing was originally created for WHITES only. Minorities were often forgotten. So, what path led, and is leading to such massive expansion? MONEY! Contracts for goods and services with the U.S. government. Union control, and redirection of money in kickbacks to campaigns.

Quality of life

The present model and integration of services in Public Housing have created a subset and false reality. Poor people are made comfortable; they are allotted so many tethered goodies to bind them to their poor status. A system that pays rent, utilities, provides some cash assistance, covers medical, dental, and vision. Some Housing Authorities are extremely progressive in deliverables and are the gatekeepers keeping Black and Brown people entrenched.

In numerous metropolitan cities Housing Authorities, which by the way there are presently 3,400 public housing authorities (PHAs), this represents billions of taxpayer dollars. Though we have to conclude people in the communities governed by PHAs must take personal responsibility to connect themselves as opportunities are presented to get OUT! The system is not designed to enrich life to thrive . . . too many giveaways tether the unconscious and keep coffers rich.

Nevertheless, what this equates to is over 5 million people directly connected to a system of POVERTY. This is cancer to the human spirit, deprives individual genius, thwarts greatness, and cheats society. Individual gifts and talents are bestowed to make a difference, to empower, and enrich society. Agencies systematically funded by governments that guarantee complacency robs the world of vision and wealth.

Negating trends

One of many dichotomies in providing services to "supposedly" eradicate homelessness is the frivolous manner in which people are placed. For instance, some intellectually challenged individuals that are mistakenly evaluated or struggle with a substance issue should never be placed in Housing Units where there are families with very small children. There is too much liability and often leads to increased social ills taking place, open use of drugs, alcohol, or the sale thereof.

Research over a few decades has shown that poverty in the United States has a range of detrimental effects on the well-being and future opportunities of residents of those areas.

Social scientists also focused on the possible theoretical causes of both the positive and negative effects of neighborhoods. For example, Galster and Killen (1995) noted the complexity of the causal influences linking metropolitan and neighborhood-based opportunities; they point out the dynamic nature of opportunities and the critical issue of resident's willingness and ability to take advantage of contextually positioned resources. A.K.A. "free stuff".

Several other social scientists offered an assessment on the harmful impact on children and teenagers living in concentrated poverty neighborhoods, and how likely their environment will adversely affect their behavior and diminish future opportunities to move beyond the traps of poverty.

Data shows from Gautreaux's results (findings) that the concerns were increasing about the high levels of racial and economic isolation of many Public Housing families. This assessment led Congress to initiate a demonstration program aimed at offering better neighborhood opportunities to Public Housing residents living in distressed inner-city areas.

Many of the findings were startling: It was recorded those isolating poor persons in inner-city ghettos and barrios does not help them connect to the rising demand for more workers

43

throughout the local regional labor markets… Also, federal, state, and local governments were found to misappropriate taxpayer's money by limiting housing and job-training subsidies to particular projects or places public or private rather than empowering poor families to choose for themselves where best to live and learn to find new and better employment by giving subsidies directly to them in lieu of agencies to decide.

Shortcomings of Prior Research

Gautreaux's research and most other research on neighborhood effects (Mayer and Jencks 1989; Crane 1991; Case and Katz 1991; Lehman and Smeeding 1997, p. 262). Jencks and Mayer (1990, p. 119) caution: The most fundamental problem confronting anyone who wants to estimate neighborhood's effects on children is distinguishing between neighborhood effects and family effects. This means that children who grow up in rich neighborhoods would differ to some extent from children who grow up in poor neighborhoods even if neighborhoods had no effect whatsoever. People typically select their neighborhoods to match their needs and resources.

Therefore, researchers restricted to cross-sectional, nonexperimental evidence must try to separate the impact of personal factors affecting the choice of a neighborhood from the effects of the neighborhood. But it is difficult—if not impossible—to measure all these socioeconomic, personal, and local characteristics well enough to distinguish their effects. The answers sought are often hidden in unmeasured factors and unexplained variations. Issues of selection bias notably limited the credibility of the findings from the Gautreaux research. First, there was evidence that families self-selected to participate in the program. There was also evidence that the program screened participants for suitability to particular neighborhoods or communities.

In the early years of Gautreaux, for example, program managers and counselors identified the families with the potential to succeed in the suburbs and matched them with landlords and communities there. Other families, judged to be less suitable for suburban locations, were not placed by the program or were placed in city neighborhoods. Second, because of the limited information gathered and kept about the families who joined Gautreaux but did not move, the differences in families' demographic or personal characteristics that affected success in moving could not be investigated. Third, some evidence of positive mobility effects in the Gautreaux program is based upon small, nonrepresentative fractions of the families enrolled—those who could be found several years later (Popkin, Buron, Levy, and Cunningham 2000). The direct solution to the problem of selectivity bias is to remove people's ability to select their neighborhoods by randomly assigning them to a community.

This detaches the individual's characteristics and preferences from the neighborhoods' potential impacts

(Brooks-Gunn, Duncan, Leventhal, and Aber 1997, p. 286). Jencks and Mayer (1990, p. 119) describe this requirement:

From a scientific perspective, the best way to estimate neighborhood effects would be to conduct controlled experiments in which we assigned families randomly to different neighborhoods, persuaded each family to remain in its assigned neighborhood for a protracted period, and then measured each neighborhood's effects on the children involved. However, until MTO, there had never been an initiative to design and implement this type of controlled experiment.

So, what have we changed? The Public Housing industry is yet expanding, budgets are increased to match the demand, but less investment is made to move families out of the system to create a bigger tax base that could offset some of the decades of waste in Public Housing.

Chapter 6

Historical Facts

Models, disparities, and everything remains the same

Housing in the 1970s

Experimental Housing Allowance Program (the end of the beginning) . . . The Housing Act of 1970 established the Experimental Housing Allowance Program (EHAP), a lengthy investigation into the potential market effects of housing vouchers. Vouchers, initially introduced in 1965, were an attempt to subsidize the demand side of the housing market rather than the supply side by supplementing a household's rent allowance until they were able to afford market rates. EHAP was designed to test three aspects of the impact of vouchers:

- **Demand:** Investigated user dynamics, including mobility, participation rates, rental rates, and housing standards.
- **Supply:** Monitored the market response to the subsidy, namely whether it changed the construction or rent rates for the community, writ large.
- **Administration:** Examined several different approaches to structuring and managing the programs.

Ultimately, new legislation on Housing Vouchers did not wait for the conclusion of the experiment. When the program concluded over a decade later, it was discovered that the program had minimal impact on surrounding rents but did have the potential to tighten the market for low-income housing, and communities were in need of an infusion of additional units. Some, therefore, argued that Public Housing was the appropriate model for cost and supply-chain reasons, though vouchers did not appear to overly distort local housing markets.

Housing Moratorium

In 1973, President Richard Nixon halted funding for numerous Housing projects in the wake of concerns regarding the housing projects constructed in the prior two decades. HUD Secretary George Romney declared that the moratorium would encompass all money for Urban Renewal and Model Cities programs, all subsidized housing, and Section 235 and 236 funding. An intensive report was commissioned from the National Housing Policy Review to analyze and assess the federal government's role in housing. This report, entitled Housing in the Seventies was instrumental in crafting new housing legislation the following year.

In keeping with Nixon's market-based approach, as demonstrated by EHAP, Nixon also lifted the moratorium on the Section 23 Voucher program late in September, allowing for 200,000 new households to be funded. The full moratorium was lifted in the summer of 1974, as Nixon faced impeachment in the wake of Watergate.

Housing and Community Development Act of 1974

The Housing and Community Development Act of 1974 created the Section 8 Housing Program to encourage the private sector to construct affordable homes. This kind of housing assistance assists poor tenants by giving a monthly subsidy to their landlords. This assistance can be 'project-based,' which applies to specific properties, or 'tenant-based,' which provides tenants with a Voucher they can use anywhere Vouchers are accepted. Tenant based Housing Vouchers covered the gap between 25% of a household's income and established fair market rent. Virtually no new project-based Section 8 housing has been produced since 1983, but tenant-based Vouchers are now the primary mechanism of assisted housing.

The other main feature of the Act was the creation of the *Community Development Block Grant (CDBG)*. While not directly tied to Public Housing, CDBGs were lump sums of money, the amount of which was determined by a formula focusing on population, given to state and local governments for housing and community development work. The sum could be used as determined by the community, though the legislation also required the development of Housing Assistance Plans (HAP) which required local communities to survey and catalog their available housing stock as well as determine the populations most in need of assistance. These were submitted as part of the CDBG application.

Again, in response to the growing discontent with Public Housing, urban developers began looking for alternate forms of affordable, low-income housing. From this concern sprang the creation of scattered-site housing programs designed to place smaller-scale, better-integrated Public Housing units in diverse neighborhoods. Scattered-site housing programs became popularized in the late 1970s and 1980s. Since that time, cities across the country have implemented such programs with varying levels of success.

Housing in the 1980s-1990s

Changes to Public Housing programs were minor during the 1980s. Under the Reagan administration, household contribution towards Section 8 rents was increased to 30% of household income and fair market rents were lowered. Public Assistance for housing efforts was reduced as part of a package of across-the-board cuts. Additionally, emergency shelters for the homeless were expanded, and homeownership by low-income families was promoted to a greater degree.

In 1990, President George H. W. Bush signed the Cranston-Gonzalez *National Affordable Housing Act (NAHA)*, which furthered the use of HOME funds for rental assistance. In his address upon its passage, Bush said, "Although the Federal Government currently serves about 4.3 million low-income families, there are about 4 million additional families, most of them very low income, whose housing needs have not been met. We should not divert assistance from those who need it most."

The next new era in Public Housing began in 1992 with the launch of the *HOPE VI program*. HOPE VI funds were devoted to demolishing poor-quality Public Housing projects and replacing them with lower-density developments, often of mixed-income.

Funds included construction and demolition costs, tenant relocation costs, and subsidies for newly constructed units. HOPE VI has become the primary vehicle for the construction of new federally subsidized units, but it suffered considerable funding cuts in 2004 under President George W. Bush.

In 1998, the Quality Housing and Work Responsibility Act (QHWRA) was passed and signed by President Bill Clinton. Following the frame of welfare reform, QHWRA developed new programs to transition families out of Public Housing, developed a homeownership model for Section 8, and expanded the HOPE VI program to replace traditional Public Housing units.

Social issues -- Concentrated poverty:

According to HUD's Residential Characteristic Report, the average annual income in 2013 for a resident of a Public Housing unit is $13,730. The same report classifies 68% of residents as Extremely Low Income, with the largest annual income bracket being $5,000 to $10,000, containing 32% of public housing residents.

An advertisement from the United States Housing Authority advocating for slum clearance as a solution for crime. Trends showing an increase in geographic concentration of poverty became evident by the 1970s as upper and middle-class residents vacated property in U.S. cities. Urban renewal programs led to widespread slum clearance, creating a need to house those displaced by the clearance (Massey and Kanaiaupuni 1993).

However, those in city governments, political organizations, and suburban communities resisted the creation of Public Housing units in middle and working-class neighborhoods, leading to the construction of such units around ghetto neighborhoods which already exhibited signs of poverty. Massey and Kanaiaupuni (1993) describe three sources of concentrated poverty in relation to public housing: income-requirements structurally creating areas of poverty, the reinforcement of patterns of poverty via the location of the Public Housing units, and the migration of impoverished individuals towards the Public Housing, although this effect is relatively small in comparison to the other sources.

A study of Public Housing in Columbus, Ohio, found that Public Housing has differing effects on the concentration of black poverty versus white poverty. Public Housing's effect on concentrated poverty is doubled for Blacks compared to Whites. The study further found that Public Housing tends to concentrate those who struggle the most economically into a specific area, further raising poverty levels.

A different study, conducted by Freeman (2003) on a national level, cast doubt onto the theory that Public Housing units have an independent effect on the concentration of poverty. The study found that while out-migration of the non-poor and in-migration of the poor were associated with the creation of Public Housing, such associations disappeared with the introduction of statistical controls, suggesting that migration levels were caused by characteristics of the neighborhood itself rather than the Public Housing unit.

Concentrated poverty from Public Housing units has effects on the economy of the surrounding area, competing for space with middle-class housing. Because of social pathologies incubated by Public Housing, Husock (2003) states that unit prices in surrounding buildings fall, reducing city revenue from property taxes and giving a disincentive to high-paying businesses to locate themselves in the area. He further argues that the pathologies caused by a concentration of poverty are likely to spread surrounding neighborhoods, forcing local residents and businesses to relocate.

Freeman and Botein (2002) are more skeptical of a reduction of property values following the building of Public Housing units. In a meta-analysis of empirical studies, they expected to find that when Public Housing lacks obtrusive architecture and its residents are similar to those already in the neighborhood, property values are not likely to fluctuate. However, a review of the literature yielded no definitive conclusions on the impact of Public Housing on property values, with only two studies lacking methodological flaws that had either mixed results or showed no impact.

Others are skeptical of concentrated poverty from Public Housing being the cause of social pathologies, arguing that such a characterization is a simplification of a much more complex set of social phenomena. According to Crump (2002), the term "concentrated poverty" was originally a spatial concept that was part of a much broader and complex sociological description of poverty, but the spatial component then became the overarching metaphor for concentrated poverty and the cause of social pathologies surrounding it. Instead of spatial concentration simply being a part of the broad description of social pathologies, Crump (2002) argues that the concept replaced the broad description, mistakenly narrowing the focus to the physical concentration of poverty.

Racial segregation: The HUD's 2013 The Location and Racial Composition of Public Housing in the United States report found that the racial distribution of residents within individual Public Housing units tends to be rather homogeneous, with African Americans and White residents stratified to separate neighborhoods. One trend that is observed is that Black neighborhoods tend to reflect a lower socioeconomic status and that White neighborhoods represent a more affluent demographic. More than 40% of Public Housing occupants live in predominantly Black neighborhoods, according to the HUD report. Even though changes have been made to address unconstitutional housing segregation, stigma, and prejudice around Public Housing projects are still prevalent.

Many White residents in Detroit in the 1940s strongly protested the creation of new Public Housing units. When their protests did not help, they left for the suburbs, also known as White flight.

Segregation in Public Housing has roots in the early developments and activities of the Federal Housing Administration (FHA), created by the Housing Act of 1934. The FHA institutionalized a practice by which it would seek to maintain racially homogenous neighborhoods through racially restrictive covenants - an explicitly discriminatory policy written into the deed of a house. This practice was struck down by the Supreme Court in 1948 in Shelley v. Kraemer because it violates the Equal Protection Clause of the 14th Amendment. However, according to Gotham (2000), Section 235 of the Housing Act of 1968 encouraged white flight from the inner city, selling suburban properties to Whites and inner-city properties to Blacks, creating neighborhoods that were racially isolated from others.

White flight - White people moving out of neighborhoods that have become more racially or ethno culturally heterogeneous - is an example of how stigma and judgment around Public Housing and affordable housing resulted in a significant change in the racial demographics of urban housing. White flight is a sociological response to perceptions that racially diverse neighborhoods will decrease their home value and increase crime rates.

McNulty and Holloway (2000) studied the intersection of Public Housing geography, race, and crime in order to determine if racial differences existed in crime rates when controlled for the proximity of public housing units. The study found that "the race-crime relationship is geographically contingent, varying as a function of the distribution of public housing". This suggests that a focus on institutional causes of crime in relation to race is more appropriate than a focus on cultural differences between races being the cause of differing crime rates. Public housing units were often built in predominantly poor and Black areas, reinforcing racial and economic differences between neighborhoods.

These social patterns are influenced by policies that constructed the narrative of racially segregated housing in the 20th Century. The rebellion in Detroit in 1967 was a symptom of racial tension that was in part due to unfair housing policies. In July 1967, President Lyndon Johnson issued a commission, led by Illinois Governor Otto Kerner to determine the causes of the riots. The Kerner Commission clearly articulated that housing inequality was solely determined by explicitly discriminatory policies. It stated that "White institutions created it, white institutions maintain it, and white society condones it". The Kerner Commission blatantly condemned White institutions for creating unequal housing opportunities, specifically highlighting restrictive covenants as a cause of the American apartheid residential pattern in the city.

Martin Luther King Jr. made housing integration a key part of his civil rights campaign and one month after the publication of the Kerner Commission was published, King was assassinated. His murder instigated another wave of riots and in response, and no later than a week after the assassination of Martin Luther King Jr., Congress passed the Fair Housing Act which prohibited discrimination in housing.

However, since the Fair Housing Act was passed, housing policies restricting minority housing to segregated neighborhoods are still heavily debated because of the vague language used in the Fair Housing Act. In the 2015 Supreme Court case Texas Department of Housing and Community Affairs v. The Inclusive Communities Project, Justice Kennedy clarified that the Fair Housing Act was intended to promote equity, not just eliminate explicit acts of discrimination. Changes in both public policy and social narrative are equally necessary for establishing equitable housing opportunities for all Americans.

Health and safety: Public housing units themselves offer very few amenities to occupants, providing the minimum necessary accommodations for living. The original wording of the 1937 Housing Act meant that units were built with minimal effort in order to give amenities only slightly better than slums. The units had poor insulation, roofing, electricity, and plumbing were generally very small and built to use as few resources as possible. Turner et al. (2005) document more physical deterioration, with backlogged repairs, vandalism, cockroaches, mold, and other problems creating a generally unsafe environment for occupants. A Boston study showed that dampness and heating issues in public housing create concentrations of dust mites, mold, and fungi, which causes asthma at a rate much higher than the national average.

Other studies have been less negative in their assessments of living conditions in public housing units, showing only marginal differences caused by public housing units. The study by Fertig and Reingold (2007) concluded that of a large list of possible health effects, public housing units only seemed to affect domestic violence levels, with only a mixed effect, a mother's overall health status, and the probability of mothers becoming overweight.

Crime is also a major issue in public housing, with surveys showing high amounts of drug-related crime and shootings. Potential causes include inefficient management, which leads to problematic residents being able to stay in the unit, and inadequate policing and security. Public Housing units are far more susceptible to homicides than comparable neighborhoods, which Griffiths and Tita (2009) argue is an effect of social isolation within the units. These homicides tend to be localized within the Public Housing unit rather than around it.

Satisfaction with one's living environment is another variable affected by Public Housing. Residents of Public

Housing units and voucher holders are more likely to express higher satisfaction with their current residency than low-income renters who are not receiving government assistance. However, the study also concluded that residents of Public Housing units and Voucher holders are more likely to express lower satisfaction with the neighborhood in which they live compared to low-income renters. This suggests that while the accommodations of Public Housing are better than comparable options, the surrounding neighborhoods are less desirable and have not been improved by government assistance.

Education: Another concern about Public Housing is the availability of quality education for children living in public housing units in areas of concentrated poverty. In a study of student achievement in New York City, Schwartz et al. (2010) found that those children living in Public Housing units did worse on standardized tests than others who go to the same or comparable schools. Furthermore, the study found that the resources of the schools serving different populations of the city were roughly the same.

Other studies refute this result, stating that Public Housing does not have a unique effect on student achievement. In a study for the National Bureau of Economic Research, Jacob (2003) found that children who had moved out of Public Housing due to demolition in Chicago fared no better and no worse in school and often continued to attend the same school as before demolition.[36] However, among older children (14 years or older), dropout rates increased by 4.4%

after demolition, though this effect was not seen in younger children.

A separate study conducted by Newman and Harkness (2000) produced findings similar to Jacob (2003). It concluded that Public Housing did not have an independent effect on educational attainment levels. Instead, variation in educational attainment was associated with poor economic standing and characteristics of the family. Additionally, the study found extraordinarily little difference between educational attainment in public versus subsidized private housing developments.

More positive educational outcomes have been recorded in other analyses. A study by Currie and Yelowitz (1999) found that families living in public housing were less likely to experience overcrowding in their units. Children living in Public Housing were 11% less likely to be held back a grade, suggesting that Public Housing may help low-income students. A 2011 report from the Center for Housing Policy argued for the benefits of stable and affordable housing in regard to education. Reasons for such educational benefits included less sporadic moving, community support, reduction in stress from overcrowding, fewer health hazards, provision of after-school programs, and reduction of homelessness.

Public perception: Several negative stereotypes associated with Public Housing create difficulties in developing new units. Tighe (2010) reviewed a breadth of literature on perceptions of Public Housing and found five major public concerns: a lack of maintenance, expectation of crime, disapproval of housing as a handout, reduction of property values, and physical unattractiveness. While the reality of certain aspects may differ from the perceptions, such perceptions are strong enough to mount formidable opposition to Public Housing programs.

In a separate study, Freeman and Botein (2002) found four major areas of public concern related to Public Housing: reduction in property values, racial transition, concentrated poverty, and increased crime. The study concludes that such concerns are only warranted in certain circumstances, and in varying degrees. While negative consequences have the potential to occur with the building of public housing, there is an almost equal chance of Public Housing having the opposite effect of creating positive impacts within the neighborhood.

Alternative models: Scattered-site housing; "Scattered-site" or "scatter site" refers to a form of housing in which publicly funded, affordable, low-density units are scattered throughout diverse, middle-class neighborhoods. It can take the form of single units spread throughout the city or clusters of family units.

Scattered-site housing can also be managed by private not-for-profit organizations using a permanent, supportive housing model, where specific barriers to the housing of the low-income individual or family are addressed in regular visits with a case manager. In New York City, The Scatter Site Apartment Program provides city contracts to not-for-profits from the HIV/AIDS Services Administration under the New York City Human Resources Administration. Also, Scattered Site is one of two models, the other being Congregate, which are utilized in the New York/New York housing agreements between New York City and New York State.

Background: Scattered-site housing units were originally constructed as an alternative form of Public Housing designed to prevent the concentration of poverty associated with more traditional high-density units. The benchmark class-action case that led to the popularization of scattered-site models was Gautreaux v. Chicago Housing Authority in 1969. Much of the motivation for this trial and lawsuit stemmed from concerns about residential segregation. It was believed that the placement of Public Housing facilities in primarily Black neighborhoods perpetuated residential segregation. The lawsuit was finally resolved with a verdict mandating that the Chicago Housing Authority redistribute Public Housing into non-black neighborhoods. U.S. District Court Judge Richard B. Austin mandated that three Public Housing units be built in white areas (less than 30% black) for every one-unit built-in Black areas (more than 30% Black).

These percentages have decreased since then and a wide array of programs have developed across the United States. While some programs have seen great successes, others have had difficulties in acquiring the land needed for construction and in maintaining new units. Eligibility requirements, generally based on household income and size, are common in these programs. In Dakota County, Minnesota, for example, eligibility ranges from a maximum of $51,550 for two people to $85,050 for 8-10 people.

Eligibility requirements are designed to ensure that those most in need receive relief first and that concerns regarding housing discrimination do not extend into the public housing sector. Public policy and implications Scattered-site housing programs are generally run by the city housing authorities or local governments. They are intended to increase the availability of affordable housing and improve the quality of low-income housing while avoiding problems associated with concentrated subsidized housing. Many scattered-site units are built to be similar in appearance to other homes in the neighborhood to somewhat mask the financial stature of tenants and reduce the stigma associated with public housing.

An issue of great concern with regards to the implementation of scattered-site programs is where to construct these housing units and how to gain the support of the community. Frequent concerns of community members include potential decreases in the retail price of their home, a decline in neighborhood safety due to elevated levels of crime.

Thus, one of the major concerns with the relocation of scattered-site tenants into white, middle-class neighborhoods is that residents will move elsewhere – a phenomenon known as white flight. To counter this phenomenon, some programs place tenants in private apartments that do not appear outwardly different. Despite these efforts, many members of middle-class, predominantly

White neighborhoods have fought hard to keep Public Housing out of their communities.

American sociologist William Julius Wilson has proposed that concentrating low-income housing in impoverished areas can limit tenants' access to social opportunity. Thus, some scattered-site programs now relocate tenants in middle-class suburban neighborhoods, hoping that immersion within social networks of greater financial stability will increase their social opportunities.

However, this strategy has not necessarily proved effective, especially with regards to boosting employment. When placed in neighborhoods of similar economic means, studies indicate that low-income residents use neighbors as social resources less often when living scattered throughout a neighborhood than when living in small clusters within a neighborhood.

There are also concerns associated with the financial burden that these programs have on the state. Scattered-site housing provides no better living conditions for its tenants than traditional concentrated housing if the units are not properly maintained. There are questions as to whether or not scattered-site public facilities are more expensive to manage because dispersal throughout the city makes maintenance more difficult.

Inclusionary Affordable Housing Program: Inclusionary zoning ordinances require housing developers to reserve a percentage between 10-30% of housing units from new or rehabilitated projects to be rented or sold at a below-market rate for low and moderate-income households. According to the United States Department of Housing and Urban Development (HUD), market-rate projects help to develop diverse communities and ensure access to similar community services and amenities regardless of socioeconomic status. Most inclusionary zoning is enacted at the municipal or county level. For example, San Francisco's Planning Code Section 415 (set forth the requirements and procedures for the Inclusionary Affordable Housing Program) "requires residential projects of 10 or more units to pay an Affordable Housing Fee, or to provide a percentage of units as affordable "on-site" within the project or "off-site" at another location in the city (Planning Code § 415, 419)."

Vouchers: Main article: Section 8 (housing)

Housing vouchers, now one of the primary methods of subsidized housing delivery in the United States, became a robust program in the United States with the passage of the 1974 Housing and Community Development Act. The program, colloquially known as Section 8, currently assists more than 1.4 million households. Through the voucher system, direct-to-landlord payments assist eligible households in covering the gap between market rents and 30% of the household's income.

Hope VI: The Hope VI program, created in 1992, was initiated in response to the physical deterioration of Public Housing units. The program rebuilds housing projects with an emphasis on mixed-income developments rather than projects which concentrate poorer households in one area.

Other City programs:

Chicago: The class-action lawsuit of Gautreaux v. CHA (1966) made Chicago the first city to mandate scattered-site housing as a way to desegregate neighborhoods. Dorothy Gautreaux argued that the Chicago Housing Authority discriminated based on race in its Public Housing policy. The case went to the Supreme Court as Hills v. Gautreaux, and the 1976 verdict mandated scattered-site housing for residents currently living in Public Housing in impoverished neighborhoods.

Since that time, scattered-site housing has become a major part of public housing in Chicago. In 2000, the Chicago Housing Authority created the Plan for Transformation designed to not only improve the structural aspects of public housing but also "build and strengthen communities by integrating public housing and its leaseholders into the larger social, economic, and physical fabric of Chicago". The goal is to have 25,000 new or remodeled units and to have these units indistinguishable from surrounding housing.

While properly run scattered-site public housing units greatly improve the quality of life of the tenants, abandoned and decrepit units foster crime and perpetuate poverty. The Chicago Housing Authority began demolishing units deemed unsafe, but the Plan for Transformation set aside $77 million to clean up sites not demolished in this process.

Houston: The Historic Oaks of Allen Parkway Village in Fourth Ward, Houston.

The Houston Housing Authority has created the Scattered Sites Homeownership Program to promote homeownership amongst those who would otherwise not be able to afford it. The program delineates strict requirements based on 80% of the Houston area's median income. In 1987, the HHA received 336 properties throughout the city, and it has worked to clean up these properties or sell them as low-cost housing. As of 2009, the HHA had helped 172 families achieve homeownership through the scattered-site program and with the properties received in 1988.

Seattle: The Seattle Housing Authority created its Scattered Site program in 1978. The program to date has a total of 800 units that range from duplex to multi-family. The program is currently in the process of "portfolio realignment," which entails successive upgrading of over 200 units and a continued effort to distribute public housing in various neighborhoods throughout the city. In choosing site locations, proximity to public facilities such as schools, parks, and transportation, is considered.

San Francisco: In 1938, the San Francisco Board of Supervisors established the San Francisco Housing Authority (SFHA), making it today one of the oldest housing authorities in California. The Housing Choice Voucher Program (formerly Section 8) was adopted in 1974 by the SFHA, and today it serves over 20,000 residents of San Francisco. Primary funding for the SFHA program comes from the U.S Department of Housing and Urban Development (HUD) and the rents paid by the housing choice voucher participants. Participants pay approximately 30 percent of their earned income for rent.

The binding thread in each program is poor people; individuals and families that were fed into a pipeline of mediocrity and marginalized to live substandard though so many opportunities exist. We have to conclude the models are broken, the investment in the product/service (social service and public housing) doesn't work effectively in spite of the billions spent annually by taxpayers. We are automatically underwriting an operational subgroup that is expanding with no end in sight and cannot continue dismissing the staggering numbers of dependent people. Presently, over 5 million individuals are tagged and caged in the system that breeds regression, and sadly is impacting increasingly more Black and Brown families that will adversely affect generations for years to come.

Chapter 7

Untethered

It is startling to learn that our government allows the Public Housing Authority to grade itself for efficiency, deliverables, and overall success, and then in spite of the grades, rewards it with more money to repeat previous cycles of ineffectiveness within the operation that aren't designed to do anything but maintain. And we all know the adage *"a fox watching the hen house is never a good thing"* and neither is the insane process by which Public Housing Authorities are allowed to operate. For decades taxpayers' adamant protests against the existence of this agency have been and remain a visual of callousness for citing the disruption public housing induces into society, as well as creating a sub outlet for gang-related activities, drug sales, and the furtherance of the miseducation of uneducated poor folks.

By HUD's own recognition in several reports cited there needs to be a sweeping overhaul in management to the private sector to better serve the vulnerable residents in its system. Obviously, there is material weakness, and that spells waste. In a snippet of a letter addressed to Congresswoman Maxine Waters of California, the US Government Accountability Office sited:

February 20, 2018,

The Honorable Maxine Waters Ranking Member Committee on Financial Services House of Representatives

Dear Ms. Waters, in 2011, the Department of Housing and Urban Development (HUD) reported that its public housing stock had approximately $25.6 billion in backlogged capital needs, with an average repair need of about $23,365 per unit, and according to HUD these figures have increased since then. HUD's Rental Assistance Demonstration (RAD) program was created, in part, to address these capital needs. Under the traditional public housing program, public housing agencies (PHA) generally cannot use private funding sources to address the capital needs of their properties. Furthermore, HUD estimates 10,000 units of public housing are demolished or disposed of each year due to disrepair.

Congress has underfunded the Agency for decades but continues to allow enrollment in spite of the financial shortfalls. It's the band-aid that continues to fall off, and the public message is "PHA" is helping families from falling through the cracks."

Though there are several programs within its purview to help provide self-sufficiency such as the **Family Self-Sufficiency Program Services (FSS)** that is designed to empower families to improve their quality of life. However, considering the number of adult residents in its system the success rate of participation is miserable. By its own definition and scope of services, it is easy to see where the pitfalls are. First, it is a voluntary program.

"Participation in the Family Self-Sufficiency (FSS) Program is voluntary for families and is open to the Public Housing and Housing Choice Voucher Program participants. Families entering the FSS Program work with an FSS Coordinator to develop goals and a plan of action to reach these goals, which will extend over a 5-year period, and lead to self-sufficiency".

One would have to question the effectiveness of this program since the agency has the autonomy to grade its own performance, and the program is voluntary so that leaves another gaping hole sucking up taxpayers' money. Many lawmakers, private citizens, and philosophers view the social agency as more of a nuisance than a benefit to society and a waste of human talent and intellect.

The Grading System

Can you imagine employees being allowed to give themselves whatever assessment they deem suitable during an evaluation? Who would ever complain about things that went wrong or give themselves a demerit for tardiness, being poorly unorganized, uncooperative, and inefficient? And not to mention, consistently lose the company's money. The self-policing policy HUD put in place with Public Housing Authorities only increased its negligence, mismanagement, and fraud. Despite having the ability to not only grade its own performance, but many officials also allowed housing properties to fall in disrepair even though they have control to manage the upkeep of facilities.

In 2019, HUD Secretary Ben Carson looked into the possibility of moving management from government agencies and assigning to private industry. It was public knowledge that Carson supported the expansion of the Obama-era Rental Assistance Demonstration program, which transfers public housing to private management. Carson felt private management would serve more effectively and eliminate a large percentage of wasteful spending and practices. Though he laid the blame at the feet of legislators for the financial shortfall.

In 2019, the agency had an astonishing $35 billion repair backlog. Roofs are leaking, boilers are breaking, and facades are collapsing across the country in buildings that provide shelter for more than 1.2 million low-income households. In body count, that's over 3.5 million individuals living in a housing system that's funded by taxpayers and controlled by Union workers, but the work is lacking. C'mon. This reek of gross mismanagement and overspending and one of many reasons why American taxpayers see no end in sight to making this a temporary stopover for families instead of the endless cycle of no return where generation after generation are stuck.

The Moving to Work Plan is intertwined in the agency's objectives to provide, improve, modernize, and preserve their public housing communities.

It reads well on paper, but the primary beneficiary is the Unions. Work is moved to keep Union trades funded, and families in power, and this only further contaminates the pool of murkiness. At some point, taxpayers have to leverage their influence and insist legislators commit to reforming this agency, along with others, that religiously fail at their tenets, and stop succumbing to the taunts of sympathizers and well-coordinated thieves who compromise the process. The blockage of legislation, circumventing of rules keep themselves untethered from rules and regulations. This is how they steal.

If there ever was an opportunity for the citizenry of the United States to create a Physical flogging agency to dole out punishment to Officials in government for wastefulness, there would not be any openings. The blatant underperformance of officials, staffing, contractors, and subs along with the countless untethered procedures that are allowed to exist is not only diminishing to the human spirit but is a blueprint for criminality.

In an article released in March 2020 submitted by writer Jacqueline Thomas, in the "Mirror", a Connecticut newspaper the heading is a nightmare:

"Local Housing Authorities Give Themselves Perfect Scores. Renters Disagree".

The subject matter highlights a mixed bag of sentiments:

Nine in 10 local Housing Authorities say they're doing well at helping the poor find housing in nice areas. But those who use Section 8 vouchers say the process is "hell."

In her article Jacqueline wrote:

"When it comes to helping low-income people find housing outside struggling neighborhoods, the federal government lets local housing authorities grade themselves on their success.

And despite data showing the poor have great difficulty finding housing in nicer neighborhoods, authorities say they're doing amazingly well.

For each of the last five years, at least 90% of local housing authorities nationwide gave themselves a perfect score in this regard, according to an analysis by The Connecticut Mirror and ProPublica of information submitted to the U.S. Department of Housing and Urban Development."

Is there any wonder we continue to see a cycle of systemic marginalization being perpetuated at the expense of taxpayers, and this very process is a conduit that has destroyed lives? It's like keeping an animal alive only to slaughter later.

The **SEMAP** system (Section Eight Management Assessment Program) was created in the late 1990s at a time of diminishing HUD staffing. The idea was that the grading system would direct the federal agency to the local housing agencies in need of improvement.

HUD's Office of Inspector General found that this reliance on self-assessment was one of the top challenges facing the vast agency. "These self-assessments are not always accurate, questioning the reliability of the information in [HUD's] systems," the office found. It's an issue the office also flagged in 2012.

To read the bottom line one could take away the inability of Public Housing Authorities failure to capture accurate analytics is sloppy, dishonest, and inefficient. Almost a deliberate methodology of dysfunction. And not to omit the other grave offenders, the Unions, it is a syndicate that takes no prisoners and exclusively divides the spoils of taxpayers hard-earned money among the family/brotherhood:

- ❖ **Boilermakers**
- ❖ **Carpenters**
- ❖ **Electrical**
- ❖ **Painters**
- ❖ **Bricklayers/Masons/Craftworkers**
- ❖ **Tile Contractors**
- ❖ **Pointers, Cleaners and Caulkers Contractors**

Considering the number of subgroups tied to these operations and the makeup of Unions, they believe in keeping it in the family, we would need to factor in the set-asides for uncles, nephews, cousins, boyfriends, and wives to direct business from the contract awards. POVERTY is a lucrative commodity.

For Fiscal Year 2021, President Trump requests $47.9 billion to support the Department of Housing and Urban Development (HUD)'s efforts to provide safe, decent, and affordable housing for the American people while being good stewards of taxpayer dollars.

A Sample Model: Philadelphia's Agency

The FY 2021 Annual Plan incorporates HUD's current reporting requirements as detailed in the HUD Form 50900, and the course of PHA's participation in the Move To Work (MTW) program that entails restructured and modified programming requirements. MTW Long-Term Goals and Objectives PHA established five (5) broad objectives in its first MTW Annual Plan:

- Reform the existing Housing Choice Voucher and Public Housing Programs
- to improve and increase the supply of quality affordable housing throughout the City of Philadelphia.
- Revitalize neighborhoods where MTW and MTW-eligible residents reside.
- Develop a MTW Family Program to furnish comprehensive family self-sufficiency services to eligible MTW families.
- Establish a Quality-of-Life Program to promote a living environment that fosters community values, encourages resident participation and positive peer group pressure and reinforces the responsibilities of public housing residents, voucher participants,

voucher landlords, and PHA to one another and to the broader community.

The aforementioned is a cyclic process that continues to require more money and considering that just 2 years ago, in 2018 PHA was allocated $161.8 million by The U.S. Department of Housing & Urban Development in Capital funds for Pennsylvania Housing Authorities to improve, modernize, and preserve their public housing communities. This is in addition to its annual operating budget of $371 million. So, imagine what the quality of life would be if investments included higher education, equally as much as they guarantee The Moving to Work model (MTW) that keeps Unions well-oiled and funded?

The Numbers

The President's Budget bolsters HUD's efforts to break the cycle of poverty by requesting $190 million for Self-Sufficiency Programs. These funds directly support key initiatives like our Family Self-Sufficiency Program, which has over 70,000 active participant households and 5,409 graduates who no longer require Temporary Assistance for Needy Families, and more than half graduate with an average savings of $6,700. Our Jobs-Plus Program is geared toward increasing employment opportunities and earnings of public housing residents through a three-pronged approach of employment services, rent-based work incentives, and community support. Through Jobs-Plus, nearly 1,500 individuals have been continuously employed for at least 180 days after placement, and residents have saved over $21.3 million in rent.

Considering there are over 5 million in the Public Housing system in the United States, these numbers are extremely disparaging. We are throwing money in the ocean and expecting to see a massive transformation when poverty is not decreasing but escalating.

As the funding hole for public housing has grown wider, HUD has begun to lean on the Rental Assistance Demonstration (RAD), an Obama-era program that transfers public housing to private management. This initiative, essentially an elaborate workaround, allows housing agencies to find the money for badly needed repairs outside of congressional appropriations. A new HUD report released last week shows that it has generated billions of dollars.

But the growth of the RAD program also reveals the shortcomings of a housing policy that relies on private companies to shelter vulnerable people. Until legislators give HUD the money it needs, millions of Americans who live in public housing will remain at risk of being displaced or priced out.

The following are the twelve priorities identified in the Strategic Directions Plan, which continue to provide a framework for PHA's activities and resource allocation in FY 2021 and beyond. PHA is in the process of updating these priorities, and will provide further information in future MTW Plans and Reports:

1. Preserve and expand the supply of affordable housing available to Philadelphia's residents with low incomes

2. Achieve excellence in the provision of management and maintenance services to PHA residents

3. Create safe communities in collaboration with neighborhood residents and law enforcement agencies

4. Enhance resident well-being and independence through partnerships for employment, job training, education, health, and other evidence-based supportive services

5. Improve access to quality housing choices and opportunity neighborhoods through the Housing Choice Voucher program

6. Incorporate energy conservation measures and sustainable practices throughout PHA operations

7. Improve customer service, streamline operations and create a business model that is data-driven and high performing

8. Conduct PHA business in an open and transparent manner that promotes accountability and access, ensures diversity, and adheres to the highest ethical standards

9. Strengthen existing relationships and forge new public, private and philanthropic partnerships to support PHA's strategic goals

10. Make PHA an employer of choice with an accountable, diverse, trained and productive workforce

11. Ensure that PHA is a good neighbor and reliable community partner

12. Encourage innovation and promote PHA's financial health through ongoing participation in the Moving To Work Program

All the aforementioned is a construct of herding; everything these Union-affiliated activities does correlates to individuals being marginalized or repeating a biopsychological model. Meaning the behavior seen and experienced in a family setting is often repeated without intervention and course-correction.

Chapter 8

153 Years of America's Housing History

The Effects of Site Control

From the first tenement regulation to work requirements for public-housing residents, these are key moments in housing policy.

1867: The first tenement-law regulation in America is enacted in New York City to ban the construction of rooms without ventilators and apartments without fire escapes.

1923: Under Mayor Daniel Hoan of the Socialist Party, Milwaukee completes construction of the country's first public-housing project.

1926: New York State passes the Limited Dividend Housing Companies Act, the first significant effort in the country to offer any kind of subsidy for affordable housing.

1934: The National Housing Act establishes the Federal Housing Administration, which insures mortgages for small, owner-occupied suburban homes as well as private multi-family housing.

1937: Congress passes the Housing Act of 1937. Originally intended to create public housing for poor and middle-income families, it is whittled down to apply only to low-income people.

1942: The Emergency Price Control Act establishes federal rent control for the first time. By January 1945, Scranton, Pennsylvania, was the only city of more than 100,000 residents with unregulated rents.

1944: The GI Bill provides mortgage-loan guarantees for home purchases by veterans.

1955: New York State introduces the Mitchell-Lama program, which subsidizes the construction of over 105,000 apartments for moderate- and middle-income residents.

1965: Congress establishes the Department of Housing and Urban Development (HUD) in a largely symbolic move to bring housing and slum-clearance programs to the cabinet level.

1968: Congress passes the Fair Housing Act, which outlaws' discrimination in housing and in mortgage lending.

1973: The Nixon administration issues a moratorium on almost all subsidized-housing programs.

1974: The Housing and Community Development Act of 1974 establishes Section 8 housing programs as a replacement for public housing.

1976: The Supreme Court rules, in Hills v. Gautreaux, that the Chicago Housing Authority contributed to racial segregation in Chicago through discriminatory practices. HUD begins offering vouchers in the city to address poverty and segregation.

1982: Under Ronald Reagan, HUD's budget is slashed to under $40 billion, a decrease of more than 50 percent from 1976, when it was $83.6 billion.

1986: Reagan introduces the low-income housing tax credit, which remains the primary source of federal funding for low-cost housing today.

1992: Congress authorizes the HOPE VI urban-revitalization demonstration program to provide grants to support low-rise, mixed-income housing rather than high-rise public housing to address a severe lack of funding for repairs. Atlanta uses its funds to clear slums and construct mostly private housing, an approach copied by cities across the country.

1996: Bill Clinton announces the "one strike and you're out" initiative to evict public-housing tenants who have criminal convictions.

2005: HUD conducts its first official point-in-time count of homeless people in the country.

2007: The housing market crashes. Nearly 3 million homes are foreclosed on in both 2009 and 2010.

2012: The Obama administration creates the Rental Assistance Demonstration program, which authorizes the transformation of public housing into private-sector Section 8 housing.

2012: The Section 8 waiting lists stretch so long that nearly half of them are simply closed.

2018: HUD Secretary Ben Carson proposes raising the rent for tenants in subsidized housing as well as enabling public-housing authorities to impose a work requirement

Whether it's plain ol' political malfeasance, rising housing costs, corporate health care, it's easy to see the looming crisis becoming nothing but catastrophic if legislation doesn't change.

Where people live affect so much of their lives—their access to transportation, education, employment opportunities, and good health care. Black-White segregation has contributed significantly to the enormous wealth gap between these races, and their grossly unequal access to strong public-education opportunities.

The historic blueprint that led to housing disparity and discrimination and disempowerment got its systemic roots after slavery:

 The 1862 Homestead Act accelerated settlement of U.S. western territory by allowing any American, including freed slaves, to put in a claim for **up to 160** free acres of federal land. And during this time whites, especially poorer whites fought vehemently to prevent blacks from owning land. Free land, though there was a small registration fee required to file a claim. However, the injustice levied against free blacks was a blueprint to keep blacks in their place, in the minds of white folks that meant beneath them, and not equal to economic status. It's now 2021 not much has changed.

Government is the culprit, and the government needs to correct the problem. More than 50 years after the passage of the Fair Housing Act, Black-White segregation remains strikingly high and imposes unfair burdens on Black people even when they have the same income or education levels as Whites.

Indeed, housing segregation, which government officials engineered as a tool of White supremacy, poses one of the largest threats to racial equality in America today. A man's home is his castle and Whites through legislative processes, unjust banking regulations, and blatant racism are the primers that have blocked many people of color from having that castle and sprawling lawn of green grass.

In American politics the issue of Public Housing has/is one of the most unwelcomed conversations; the myriad of disconnects and biopsychosocial elements that factor into adverse behavior patterns that in some cases would take decades to correct, but also provides a glimpse into the damaged lives of people who are merely scratching for crumbs just to survive but are looked upon and, in some cases treated inhumanely.

The 'mythical house' of protection (Public Housing) that was constructed to prevent total social wipeout and prevent the downtrodden, poor, low-income, disabled, and sometimes abused, is the same house where the psychological disease of complacency and misinformation is unchecked and eroding the quality of life of those it swore to help. During Roosevelt's presidency, the government made a small but significant effort to serve low-income Americans. The Congress in 1933 introduced public housing in trial form as part of a public works bill and the U.S. Housing Act of 1937 set up the permanent program that still exists today.

Whilst to the external world it appears residents in public housing are just lazy, uncaring, and looking to freeload, you have thousands just hoping to strike the right chord to climb out the belly of this bottomless beast. Not all are truly comfortable being and living uncomfortably amidst crime. Blacks, and Latinas, and other people of color. But the history of public housing started with a segregated placement for whites only in Atlanta, Georgia.

Atlanta's Techwood Homes, the first public-housing project built by the PWA, in 1936, was for whites only. *(AP Photo)*

However, in spite of the Public Housing Authorities coverups, misuse, and mismanagement the government sees it as it's better than nothing; poor people have to be placed somewhere otherwise our society would be overrun with squalor.

GAO says it is more of the same . . .

The government's own evaluations also reveal shortcomings: A **GAO** report U.S. Government Accountability Office) on the program from 2016, for instance, said that "HUD needs to take action to improve ongoing oversight" into how RAD affects residents. HUD's own new report, furthermore, found that one in ten residents still noticed problems like leaks and mold after the private renovations were completed and that one in four residents didn't receive financial assistance to help with their moving expenses during construction.

But despite concerns about mismanagement and resident intimidation, many housing officials see the program as the lesser of two evils—better than doing nothing at all.

In an article written in the Prospect, we see the imminent concern that plagues every metropolitan city… a system where the money faucet is just running.

"There's just no way to get the money otherwise," says Joseph Shuldiner, director of the Yonkers housing authority, north of New York City. "You can't make up for the fact that Congress underfunds the program." Yonkers has converted nine of its 11 housing projects through RAD, which allowed officials to repair roofs, facades, and water heaters, as well as replacing windows, carpets, and appliances.

"We would have held the buildings together with masking tape for as long as we could, but the systems were failing," Shuldiner says. "We needed $180 to $200 million, and we were getting $3 million a year from Congress. You have to fix the buildings first, then you can talk about right and wrong."

Just because the program hasn't yet been catastrophic, though, doesn't mean it never could become so, and Gramlich says the

Trump administration so far seems far less interested in protecting residents than its predecessor.

"The Obama administration tapped the private sector because that's where the money is," Gramlich says. "The residents were leery, they were fearful of being displaced, but their housing was crumbling around their heads, so they knew something needed to be done. With the current administration, it's more a matter of 'we don't like public things, we like private things.'"

These concerns highlight RAD's origins as a Band-Aid for the larger problem of Congressional inaction. If the political will were there, Congress could easily provide enough funding to restore the country's public housing to a safe, livable standard. Not only that, but it could also expand assistance for low-income renters:

> **The mortgage-interest tax deduction, which subsidizes homeownership, cost the federal government three times as much money last year as the entire Section 8 voucher program.**

But decades of austerity and fearmongering about urban crime have made renters in general, and public-housing residents in particular, *personae non gratae* in American politics. It's that legacy that now forces them to rely on compromise programs like RAD to ensure the safety of the roofs above their heads.

This book was written to inspire, challenge and awaken the consciousness and convictions of lawyers, social workers, psychologists, and other behavior experts and students aspiring in any of the aforementioned disciplines to utilize this book as a current blueprint when engaging with Black and Brown people. To consider the systemic or biopsychosocial factors that are driving mental illness, adverse behavior and blocks progress and as necessary to become advocates and leaders of social change and step up to lobby change in legislation that could possibly overhaul a system that was constructed to contain the herd and restricts human evolvement.

ABOUT THE AUTHOR

Melvin Prince Johnakin Jr.

He has served as a Project Manager for one of the City of Philadelphia's Public Housing HOPE VI redevelopment projects valued at $52 million. Mr. Johnakin's involvement forced the local Housing Authority, property developers, and general contractors to actively engage in the training and hiring of residents, in accord with Section 3 of the Housing and Urban Development Act of 1968, as amended. He has attracted the ears of those in local government by bringing a source of reason and advocacy to the cause of economic development in distressed communities; this includes testifying before the Philadelphia City Council on multiple occasions. He has served as an economic development consultant for Universal Community Homes, a multi-million-dollar community development enterprise started by world-renowned music composer and legend, Mr. Kenny Gamble.

His professional affiliations include but are not limited to: Omega Psi Phi Fraternity, Inc., Mason Hiram #5 and Shriner Pyramid #1. Additionally, he has been presented with numerous community service awards including the *Men Making a Difference Award*, presented by the former U.S. Representative Chaka Fattah (D-PA).

Mr. Johnakin received a Bachelor of Science in Recreation Leisure Management (Magna Cum Laude) – minor in Sociology from Cheyney University, Cheyney, PA; a Master's Degree Business Systems (MBS) - Concentration Human Resources & Entrepreneurship, from Lincoln University, Coatesville, PA; and is a Doctoral Candidate in Business - Concentration Urban Planning, from Walden University, Baltimore, MD

www.ingramcontent.com/pod-product-compliance
Lightning Source LLC
Chambersburg PA
CBHW071112210326

41519CB00020B/6278